MW01612966

Empath Survival Guide

Reclaim the power of your emotions and living your life to the fullest with this complete guide.
Self Care handbook for Sensitive People.

Scott Wilkinson

Table of Contents

Additionally, the information in the following pages is intended only for informational purposes and should thus be thought of as universal. As befitting its nature, it is presented without assurance regarding its prolonged validity or interim quality. Trademarks that are mentioned are done without written consent and can in no way be considered an endorsement from the trademark holder.

Chapter 1: Why Is It So Hard to Recover From Narcissistic Abuse

As someone who has dealt with narcissistic abuse, it is hard to recover from all of the abuse that your partner put on you, especially because you loved and trusted them so much. Your idea of what loyalty and honesty is has been tarnished, and you aren't sure were to turn. Research confirms that divorce and breakups are always something that is difficult to go through, but coming out of a relationship, especially when it was a long term one, is going to be entirely different.

Recovery is not always going to be hard, but when you start to look into some of the intricacies, it should be easy for you to walk away from this person. When we actually take some time to look through some of the things that happened with that relationship. For example, when you look back at the relationship, you will notice that you were always being abused, psychologically, physically, and emotionally. Your partner, no matter how much they tried to tell you that they love you, they really didn't respect you for who you are, and when you spend some time thinking about it, you will find that it is easier to realize why this is such a bad thing to work with and go back to the narcissist.

But, of course, there are a lot of times when this doesn't happen. The target is not able to deal with letting go, and they are going to find that this increases the amount of time it takes to recover from the abuse. Why is it then, that targets find that it is harder to come out of a relationship that is abusive than it is to get over a breakup and divorce?

It is because you don't have what is known as the Casablanca effect. Think back to the scene in this movie where the lead actress is asked to get on to the pane with her husband, and then she asks the lead actor "What about us?" Then he says "We'll always have Paris". The lead character is able to understand why she left him earlier and comes to terms with this reality, yet he is going to feel the pain of being abandoned by the other person. But he could regain the love and the experience if he just remembered their moments in Paris.

Now, when you are working with a narcissist, this is something that is never going to happen. Because there is never really going to be a "We'll always have Paris" moment in this kind of relationship, it is hard to live through this kind of moment. This is because everything that you have ever believed about the narcissist, every promise, every moment that was spent together, and every connection isn't going to make sense here because of the betrayal that happens. You are going to have a lot of doubt that come sup here in trying to figure out if there is any reality at all in the relationship that you have.

When you finally decide to leave the relationship, and you decide to walk away from them, you are not really recovering from a failed relationship, but you are also dealing with warfare.

Love patterns of the narcissist

During this time, it is not uncommon to feel like you are unlovable. You may start to ask the question about whether the narcissist ever actually love you, even once? You may wonder if this abuser is thinking about you now? Is it possible that it was all a mistake and that they are going to come back?

It is going to be natural for you as the victim to ask these kinds of questions, and they may ask then hundreds of times in their heads. Even though the narcissist stripped you down to just a fraction of the kind of person that you used to be. They abused you in all ways possible. And they made your self-confidence and self-esteem pretty much disappear. But even with al of that, you are going to hold onto a faint hope that somewhere, even if it is a small chance, that the abuser is going to come back to you.

It is not that difficult in order to understand the patterns that these people go through because they are often going to be really predictable. Their relationship behavior is going to be pretty much the same with everyone they have been with in the past. It is easy to predict the behavior that they are going to use if you have a good idea of the love patterns that they used with their ex. This may seem a bit silly, but it is going to give you some more clarity as you begin to realize how they actually saw you, and if the relationship really meant anything at all to them.

There are going to be some love patterns that a narcissist is going to show to others. And they are often going to be really easy to see, and are going to be so common that you are going to be able to distinguish them by name pretty easily.

Some of the names and types of love patterns that come with your narcissist includes

1. The novelty seeker

2. The big game hunger

3. The white knight

4. The recycler

5. The romantic

6. The hater

Unfortunately, it is common for most of the targets to want their ex-partner if that narcissist displayed the patterns of the romantic on a regular basis. Why is the loss so distressing for women that they are going to long for this pattern, this abuser, to come back. The fact is whatever your ex-partner has told you when he was in love with you was what he actually meant to say. Yes, you read that right. You are not crazy. He really meant it when he said he loved you.

This is hard to deal with, but in reality, that abuser was in love with you. But there is a bit of a difference to deal with here. That abuser is not really in love with the true you, but he was in love with the perfect partner that they noticed in you. This is a romantic fantasy that is going to seem like both are the perfect partners.

The narcissist as a romantic is going to love the idea of having another partner who can be their part in a perfect romance. They may think about mesmerizing candlelight dinner, long car rides, moonlight walks by the beach, and even those great weekend getaways to that cabin in the woods. But remember that the goal of the narcissist is to make sure that all of the moments that the two of you have, especially in the beginning, will done to feel intimate and romantic.

The narcissist is going to work to make their target feel like they are the most lovable and beautiful person in the world. They are going to make it all sound perfect by introducing you to his friends and to his social network, and he will spend a lot of time talking about how blessed he feels to have you in his life.

And then, as soon as you start to get comfortable and feel like you have found your ideal partner, and you start to think about taking a step ahead, he is going to back off. You get to hear a lot of excuses on why they weren't able to meet when planned or call you at all. This is going to leave you feeling confused about what is going on in the relationship.

The narcissist is hoping that you will not pay attention to the feelings and emotions that you are dealing with, because they are going to use these against you. If you were in a relationship with anyone else, all of the romance and the gestures would lead to a great trust and can lead to the intimacy that a relationship needs. But when you are dealing with a narcissist, when they start to realize that the fantasy is turning into reality, they are going to get frustrated and will start to get frustrated.

If you are lucky, they are going to get annoyed and will walk away without paying any attention to your emotions. This allows you to get out with just a bit of confusion and not really understanding what happened. But in many cases, this kind of person is not going to let go. They are going to keep up with you, tormenting you in any method that they can and ensuring that your confidence is broken along the way.

I really miss them, what do I do now?

It is depressing to deal with any kind of breakup, but it is so much worse to deal with a narcissist because it is going to really test your strength and patience. You are going to get thwarted by your own boundaries, and in the long run, all that you are going to feel is every level and sort of exhaustion.

You are unable to look at this as a relationship that is completely over, mainly because you are going to continue to yearn for that person to come back to you.

Yes, the relationship is going to be over, and yes you know that it was really bad for you. And you know that you should be thankful that it is over and you never have to deal with it ever again. But, because of that romance period that happened in the beginning, you will find that all of that yearning is going to continue coming back to you over and over again. You find that things are going to be really far from reality. You may notice that there are a lot of mixed emotions that are going to overwhelm you. One moment you want that abuser back, and the next moment, you are mad at them and never want to see them again. The feelings are going to get so intense and will eventually stretch out from disgust and to desire and back and forth again. But why does this all happen?

The kind of bond that you are going to form with the narcissist during that time is going to be traumatic. Even with this though is that it is you are going to have a lot of trouble seeing the difference between fantasy and reality. This is something that specialists are going to call the trauma bond. With this kind of bone, the target is going to revisit the past so much that it is going to take up 100 percent of the energy I their brain, and it can end up with that past controlling your nervous system for years in the future.

Because of this trauma bond, your mind is going to keep on churning out all of the memories that are there, and at some point, you are going to have a lot of trouble figuring out what was in the past, and what was in the present. Because these thoughts are going to take over so much of your mind, you will find that it is hard to be in the present, and you are able to turn things around in your head.

For example, instead of being in the present, you are going to learn how to turn things around in your brain. You are able to convince yourself that this narcissist actually cares for you, and that they are thinking about you at this moment. And this isn't where it is all going to stop. It won't be long before there is a list of what-ifs that show up in your head and it is going to get harder and harder to bring yourself out of the past.

Remember, even though this trauma bond is going to be super strong, but it is not the same thing as love. However, it is going to be a form of emotional addiction. It is going to take you through a lot of different roller coaster rides that will give you the feeling of being high, just like you would with a drug or with alcohol.

This is because the narcissistic partner is going to abuse his victim with distressing arguments, spiteful insults, and they will try to intensify the fear of abandoning. It isn't going to take long before they are going to make some change sin order to do an extreme act of intimacy, soulful apologies, and even some awesome sex. This is done just often enough that the target is going to be able to feel like there is something that is actually there between them and the abuser.

So, when you start to think about all of the arguments and the fights that you and your partner had, instead of thinking about the pain that you went through, think about all of the good moments that followed it. You think about those times, and you assume that the narcissist actually cared for you, but this was not really the case for you.

The best way to hep you get through this situation Is to look at it all from the perspective of a third party, or the opinion of someone else. The moments that you remember fondly and think were romantic, were not real, and those who are not in the relationship are going to realize this better than anyone else. The feelings you are going through now, the fear, the unworthiness, and the self-doubt, were there from the beginning, and they were created by the narcissist. You just weren't able to realize it from the start.

When you allow yourself to be in love with this narcissist, it is only going to lead to more and more bad things. You are going to expose yourself to some permanent damage. The access, the love and the trust that you gave to the narcissist will allow them to sneak back into your system and is going to make things so much worse. Because of this, you are going to have to go to war with two different points of view at a time. One is going to be yours, and the other one is going to be from your narcissistic partner. Eventually, one of these will need to die out because they can't coexist at the same time.

Chapter 2: What are Some Strategies You Can Use to Finally Move On

At this point, we have taken a good look at what narcissism is all about, how the abuser is able to gain the control and the power that they want in order to influence their targets, and how the targets are going to stay in this endless cycle until they can learn more about the situation around narcissism, and then make the right steps to ensure they get better.

There are actually a few strategies that you are able to use in order to help you feel better as you go along this road of healing. This chapter is going to give you a few options that you can start on, but talking to your therapist (which we are going to talk about in a little bit) can also help you out as well. Some of the things that you can do in order to help you to get over the narcissistic relationship are going to include

Let the truth be your best friend

As a victim of the abuse, it is likely that you have spent a lot of time ignoring the truth about your ex-partner.

Sure, you looked around and noticed the issue once, but now that you are away, you often worry that you made the wrong decision, and that maybe this person still loves you and wants you back. But if you actually allowed yourself to look at the truth of the situation, rather than trying to block it all out all the time, you will see that you are just living in a fantasy land, and all you are doing in the process is harming yourself.

The first thing that you need to focus on here is letting the truth become one of your best friends. Stop fantasizing about all the things that the relationship was not, and instead focus on the reality of the situation. You need to work hard in order to make truth your new best friend, rather than worrying about what could have, might have, or should have been. You know what happened during that relationship, and now it is time to move on and not let it affect you again.

A good way to do this is to record yourself (you can use a recording device or use an app on your phone or your computer) and then record each and every thing that you are able to remember when it comes to your partner. Don't be afraid here, no one else is going to see this recorder, unless you would like them to, and it can be a great way for you to let out your feelings and really get to know why you left the person in the first place.

When you are working on this, you want to make sure that you talk about the abuses that they sent your way, the fact that they always had to abuse you and blame you for things, and all of the various ways that the abuser tried to hurt you. If you feel like it, you can go through and write down some of the information as well, or at least the bullet points, and go from there.

Once you have a list of at east the main things that the narcissist did to you, it is time to put this list somewhere you are able to see on a regular basis. Your last exercise before you do this though is to take all of the points that you just wrote, and then go through it and then write each one as a one liner. A good example of what you can do with this would include something like "The person is a leech who sucks my soul every time that he enters my life, and I am in no mood to encourage him any further"

The point of doing this list is that each time you start to feel a bit unsure about yourself when it is time to leave the relationship, and any time that you worry about the relationship and if it is time to go back, you can repeat these phrases to yourself, and help yourself to feel better.

Practice some mindfulness

It is possible for you as the abused, even though the abuser probably spent a lot of time telling you that you mean nothing and that you should be so thankful that they want to spend time with you and that you can't do anything, to break the spell of the narcissist and start to recuperate your attention with the help of some mindfulness. This is similar to the meditation that we talked about before, but it is going to be more focused on taking those same principles and moving them to all the other parts of your life as well.

While it is going to be almost impossible for you to go through and completely wipe your thoughts clean, it is possible to take a look at those thoughts, not within your own head, but from a safe and neutral point.

You won't allow the thoughts to consume you, but you will take some time to look at these thoughts like you are an observer, as someone who is seeing these things for the first time and trying to help a friend. If you are able to do this in the proper manner, then you can learn a lot of things, and the judgment is not going to be a big deal.

The first thing to do with this one is go through and write down the list of things that you wish you were able to do for yourself. It is best if you can start out with a week or so, and then come up with one or two things that you would like to do for that day.

It isn't necessary for you to go through and come up with something that is overly complicated to work with. For example, it is fine to write down something like taking some time to help nourish your soul and spend more time in the present, rather than worrying so much about the past. You may choose to spend time doing some yoga, watching your favorite movie, preparing a meal, walking the dog, and even getting a massage.

No matter what you are able to decide goes on the list, take the time to do it with all of your heart. If your mind tries to replay the thoughts that the narcissist tried to put there in the past, just remember that one liner that we had from before. Repeat it in your head, and then move on with your day.

Heal yourself with the help of reconnecting

After all that you went through while you were in that kind of relationship, it is not that uncommon for you to take some time to isolate yourself even more. Most people have no want to stay around others after they have spent some time being used , ignored, isolated, made fun of and blamed for everything that happened in that relationship. The victim is likely to feel like they are all on their own, and they are going to try and keep others at bay against them.

It is fine to take a bit of time to yourself. It is not necessary to jump right out there and start dating again, or jump out there and socialize every night of the week.

This is going to exhaust you even more than the narcissist had been able to do, and it is going to be really hard to get yourself recovered and to avoid the issues that come up with the narcissists attacking you yet once again.

It is just fine to take some time to yourself. But you do not want to end up so isolated that you are at home all day long, barely leaving for work, and only spending a bit of time socializing when you actually have to. It is a good thing for you to get out and do some socializing, this is going to help you to really open up your world, get over the bad thoughts that you are having now that the relationship is over, and makes it much harder for the narcissist to try and put one over on you.

At this point, you need to go through and click on the reset button, and allow yourself to start over the whole story from the start. At first, you are going to find that it is hard to trust yourself, and you will find that it is even harder for you to trust other people. While you don't need to go through and rush this trust or this socialization process, it is still something that you need to be considering. It is perfectly normal to take your time, and to let it all happen a bit more naturally, but make sure that you don't become a hermit, someone who is going to stay home al the time and never want to do anything with anyone else.

At this time, tell yourself that the intelligence that you possess really has nothing to do with being a victim of that abuser. It was really just was bad luck that the narcissist found you and you became their target.

The sooner that you are able to learn about this and realize it, the easier it is to find yourself and start to connect.

Just like with anyone else, all that you want in your life is to feel loved, but sometimes, especially when a narcissist starts to come into the picture and take over, it is going to not go the way that you want. Give yourself a bit of time after the relationship ends to forget and forgive yourself for falling into that relationship.

From here, take in a deep and slow breath.

Get yourself over into analyzing mode, making sure that there are not a lot of thoughts and emotions that are going on in there. try to be calm, and see if you are able to find your answers to the whys this is needed because it will ensure that you will never again fall into the trap of the narcissist, even if you meet up with thousands of them throughout your life

If you do need this, then you need to take the time to find a way to connect with your inner self. Get out of that relationship with the narcissist, the toxic relationship that you are ready to dump out, and then find yourself a simple and easy to use breathing space. The way that you do this is going to vary based on the person, but some of the things that you can try is to go out and dine with some friends you trust, getting outside with nature and with animals, and spending some time reading a book

It is only possible for you to analyze what is going on in the mid, and to make some steady progress, once your mind is clear, and all of the unwanted thoughts are gone overthinking during this time is going to be pretty dangerous to do, and it is much better to let all these thoughts go. And if these thoughts start to take over your mind, and you feel that you are sinking into a depression and going to let it all take over you, then it is time to get your mind distracted and go do things.

The more new things that you can do, and the more that you are able to get out of the house, the easier it is to keep those negative thoughts away, and to ensure that you are going to take care of yourself.

Try something new, like a new instrument, hanging with friends, painting and more. If you are able to and brave enough, you can leave that comfort zone and help yourself to break all the barriers that may have been holding you back before.

In addition, it is fine to be open to new relationships. This doesn't mean that you should just jump into a new relationship and start the process all over again. The more that you rush from one relationship to another, the easier it is for a narcissist to find you and try to target you again. But it does mean that you need to be open to some of the new people who may be brought into your life. Don't raise up a wall and shun everyone you meet, but learn to go with the flow and give it some time to grow on their own, whether it terns into a romantic relationship or they become a new friend.

Self-healing is going to be one of the most important things that you are going to do when it comes to your emotional wounds, especially when you decide to leave the abuse. If you do not take care of those wounds, it is likely that you are going to see them become raw and fresh.

Taking care of your own wounds, and working on improving and investing your energy and time now to learn more about yourself, and your behavioral patterns. Understand that all of those characteristics of the partner were used against you, and start to use these experiences as a kind of tool so that you won't fall for that trap again, either with your old partner, or with a new narcissist who tries to take you in.

And finally with this one, you need to learn how to say no to things. A lot of time the perfect target is going to be someone who has no boundaries against the narcissist, and someone who is willing to say yes and go along with everything, no matter how much they don't want to do something.

At this time, if you want to regain some control over your life, and not allow the narcissist to come back in and cause problems, then you need to learn how to say no, and practice it any time that you feel someone is trying to pressure you into doing something that you don't wish to do. Now that you are the one who gets to hold all of the keys to your life, be very careful about whom you decide to hand them over to again.

The no contact rule

As a victim of abuse, it is important to play the no contact rule.

There may be some exceptions to this, such as if you have children with the abuser and you have to share custody. But if you can help it at all, then there should be no contact between you and the narcissist once you leave the relationship. Each time that you decide to talk to the narcissist, and allow them back in is an opportunity for them to try and wiggle themselves back into your life.

The less contact that you are able to have with the narcissist, the better in most cases. The narcissist is not really wanting to get back with you because they love and care about you, no matter how many times they may say that or no matter how many times they are going to try and use some flowery words to entice you to come back. And there are times when the narcissist is going to try to make your growing self-esteem go back down, by sending you messages at every chance that they get in order to convince you that you made the wrong decision, that you are nothing without them, and that you should come back.

Yes, it is true that at one point, you did love this person. But this person never loved you, and they are very toxic for you to be around. Letting them back into your world with a lot of contact and even reading them to see if the other person still loves you or not, is going to kick down all of the hard work that you have done in the past.

Don't think that you are strong enough to avoid this person, or that you will be able to get through it all without falling the victim again. While this may sound a bit harsh in the beginning, you did fall for that person once already, why try to risk is again. You need to just turn off contact with that person as much as possible, so that you are able to get your life back on track in some manner.

If you have to, go through and see if you are able to block this person from everything. Go down to the phone store and get their number blocked.

Go online and figure out which social media sites, emails and more you are a part of, and block them as well. The narcissist is going to use every means that they can get ahold of in order to try and reach you. And each time they do, you are going to be tempted into replying and see what they say. It is much better for your mental health, and for your own resolve, to block them and never even see the messages in the first place.

Find a good support group

Another thing that you can consider doing when it comes to finally healing from the abuse that the narcissist did to you is going out there and finding a really good support group to work with.

This group is going to be the ones who are there to help guide you, to lift you up, and to make sure that you are not going to get lonely, or be destroyed by your own thoughts, when it is time to move on, rather than finding your way back to the narcissist.

There are going to be some people who you used to be close to in your life, who will now have no interest in being your support group or helping you out. This may hurt a bit, but just let it go and move on to finding people who want to help you, rather than people who may feel some kind of obligation to help you, but who don't really want to do it at all.

There are a lot of reasons why you may have lost your friends when you were with the narcissist. Some people are going to be hurt by the things that you or the narcissist said to them. Others are going to be mad that you went into isolation and had nothing to do with them for a good amount of time. it is okay for them to be hurt a bit by what happened. Let them be that way, and focus your energy on getting better and finding those who can support you now. Maybe later, when some of the wounds heal up, you will be able to work with those people and try to make amends.

Learn how to let things go

As hard as it is when you end a relationship with a narcissist, you need to be willing things go. Yes, you are angry at the narcissist and all of the things that they decided to put you through. Yes you were abused and may be tired and angry and a bunch of other things. It is fine and even normal to have these thoughts, and it is important to stop and recognize them a little bit, it is also important to remember that these things, if you hold onto them for too long or too hard.

It is best if you are able to recognize what happened in the past, and recognize that it did affect the person you are today. But once you are done with that, let it all go. There is no reason to hold all of that negative stuff.

It is just going to hold you back, and will make it hard for you to move on with your life. If you find that it is hard to let go, then it is time to find a good support group and the right therapist for your needs.

Remember the bad things, and none of the good

This one kind of sounds like we are trying to just get you to focus on the bad and feel miserable all of the time, but that is not really the intention at all. The point here is that we want you to forget all of it, but first, forget all of the good stuff. The sooner you are able to remember the few good things that happened in the relationship, the easier it is going to be for you to get over the narcissist.

One of the biggest issues that a lot of targets are going to have is with the idea of remembering the good stuff. They think about the bad stuff and get mad about what is happening or what did happen to them. But then they wait a moment and start remembering the few good things. They may even take these things and exaggerate them a bit in their own eyes.

The problem with this is that when you bring out the good things, you are going to find that it is easy to forget and forgive the bad. This makes it more likely that you are going to give in here, and run back to the narcissist the moment that you can.

This is a very dangerous thing to do. Though you my have created an alternate fantasy of the relationship, and you may think that it is going to get so much better if you just give the abuser one more chance. The problem with this is that, each time you get back into the abuse cycle, and the longer you stay there, the harder it is going to be to finally get out.

Dealing with a narcissist is hard. Even though you are probably really tired for all of the work that you have done to fight off the narcissist so far, you are going to have to keep up with this for a bit longer.

If you let your guard down here, and you don't work to really make sure that the narcissist, your abuser, has no say in your life any longer, then it is likely that the narcissist is going to try and get back into your life again and again. Follow the strategies above, and you will be able to walk away each and every time. the narcissist is going to be persistent, and they won't give up easily, but at some point, if you are able to resist them long enough, they are going to find a new target to bother, and will leave you alone.

Chapter 3: Don't Fall For the Trap of Narcissism Again

Reclaiming your mind is the first step that the target is going to take in order to help yourself recover from the abuse that you went through with your target. This is because all of the insanity that the narcissit is trying to send your way is able to come through and consume each and every aspect of your life. And it isn't going to be long before you are spending all of your time and energy working on pleasing the narcissist (and their never ending high standards are impossible to impress), and losing al of the purpose that came to your life.

You need to start straight from the bottom when you decide to end the relationship with the narcissist. You need to start by claiming what should be your birth right, which includes your own actions, thoughts, and feelings. And from there, once you have been able to reclaim these, you will need to work on fighting the narcissist in order to get your own individuality back.

This is a process that is going to take some time before you see a bunch of results about it. This can be hard because it is much nicer to see things change as quickly as possible. But in reality, this is not going to happen, especially when you are dealing with all of the issues and the tricks of the narcissist. Just know, if you continue to move towards your goals slowly and steadily, you are going to get there. and when you do, you will find that there is something shocking there. you will find that you are worthy to be loved, and that there is a good reason behind why you exist on this world, outside of trying to make the narcissist happy (which is impossible0.

All of this is going to happen when you start to heal yourself. And it is going to be something that is going to take a long time and can be really tiring, but remember that the journey is not going to be impossible. You must be determined and strong to get back on your own legs. If you are able to take yourself slowly, and not worry about how fast or slow this is all taking, you will be able to let the wounds heal and you will feel so much better.

How can I stay off the radar of the narcissist

When you are done with this kind of abusive relationship, it is easy for you to become more vulnerable, and many of the targets of this kind of situation is going to be intimidated easily.

You might also start attracting the wrong kinds of people into your life. Doing this is going to ensure that you end up with another narcissist, and this is going to ensure that the cycle will continue to go over and over again. But why does this happen?

It often takes months and even years to realize that your partner is a narcissist and that you need to be careful. You may not start to realize this for some time though, and often it is going to be someone on the outside who is trying to get in, and the target goes through research mode. When you realize that your relationship is starting to become too toxic for you and it is going to start consuming your happiness, and this is going to start to look at things from a brand new perspective.

Coming out of the relationship may not sound like a good idea if you feel that you need to do it right here and now. But you may decide to go through and do some research, and give it some time. of course though, things are just going to get worse the longer that you are in this relationship and the longer you allow it to go on. Eventually, things are going to get so bad that you give up and try to walk away.

That is an amazing thing that you were able to walk away from that bad relationship. You are working on healing and recovering yourself, but what if you are about to start repeating this same mistake again? This is definitely not something that anyone wants to deal with. Educating yourself about narcissism and all of the patterns that come with it, but you should know when it is time to stop. When you start to Google the symptoms every time that you meet a new person because you are worried about things, this is probably the time to slow down. But if you are actually worried about someone you met, and you feel that they have to be too good to be true, then it is probably time to walk away and ensure that you aren't going to get harmed in the process again.

During this time, try to make sure that those emotions are not going to be buried deep down inside you. Writing a journal is a great way to work with this. You may want to carry it along with you. This way, each time that there is a trigger that upsets you or starts to play on your emotions and pull you back to the past, you are able to write down all of the thoughts and experiences that you are dealing with, and then you are able to get them all out, without feeling like you are beating yourself up.

Any time that you are working on your journal and you start to notice that the thoughts you are writing about start to go towards one particular incident, then it is time to go through and write it all down. Whenever you feel that there is an eye-opener that is occurring in your life, then that needs to get written down in the journal as well.

For example, let's say that you are pondering over what happened in the past and thinking about the times when your abuser said that you were always selfish and worthless. Even after not being with them for some time, it is likely that you are going to feel that hurt, and you may even let it start engulfing you.

But for this time, rather than letting those emotions catch up with you and take over your day, it is time to do a bit of reality checks. Throwing those bad thoughts away and some of those negative emotions in the trash, take some time to think about all of the good things that you have seen happen in your life. Think about all the people who have called you a beautiful soul because of some kind of act that you did in the past. You are soon going to see that you are an important person, and the narcissist didn't really are for you.

Instead, they decided to use the cheapest trick in the book in order to make sure that your self-esteem went down as far as possible.

The end of any relationship isn't going to be the end of the world by any means, even though it may feel like it for some time, and maybe even for a long time depending on what the narcissist was able to convince you of, and how long you were with them.
Instead of thinking about the relationship at the end of your word, start to see it as a start to your new life. You have already done the task of self-educating yourself about narcissism and what it al means. Now it is time to take this a bit further and start to invest some more time into learning who you really are. Unless you are able to bring back the old you, then it is going to be difficult for you to get into a new relationship, simply because the only people you are going to attract to you will be narcissists.

The best thing that you are able to do when you are ready to end that relationship and protect yourself from any more narcissists entering your life, is to stop thinking that you are so unworthy of love.

This is the number one thought that is going to land anyone, whether they are a past victim or not, back into the arms of another narcissist. Regrades of how long it ends up taking, you need to start with the belief that you are worth of having lots of love in your life, and that you are allowed to live your life the way hat you would like.

During this process, never let yourself fall back into some of the negative behavioral patterns and thoughts. Each time that you are sitting there and notice that there is a negative pattern or thought coming into your mind, stop and intentionally try to swap it out for a thought that is more positive.

For example, it is easy, after leaving the abuser to feel that the self-defeating thoughts should be the ones who take over the mind and control. It is easy to fall into the trap of thinking "My ex-partner never saw anything good in me. What if I was really not good enough. Maybe I should have worked more on understanding him better. It must have really been my fault."

Always remember that it is the narcissist who has a fault here. They are going to work hard to try and blame you all the times that they can, but in reality, they are the ones who are causing the damage to the relationship and to you, they just don't really care at all.

Instead of using the thoughts that were above, you can work with the following option for self-mastery: "I did the best that I could, but the inefficiency of my ex-partner clouded his mind in seeing it. It isn't my fault anymore. I can't help if he has a deficit. Never will I allow anyone to ill-treat me again, not now and not I the future."

As you can see, the blame is going to be shifted a bit here. In the first one, you took on all the blame, just like what you were used to doing when you were with the narcissist.

This was going to serve the narcissist because they gained a lot of control over you, and because they find that they themselves can never be the one who is to blame for things that happen.

But when we decide to move to the second one, we find that we are not really to blame. We spent a lot of time and effort trying to make our partner as happy as possible. But no matter how hard we tried, it was no use. And often this is because of something that is wrong with the narcissist, rather than something that has anything to do with the target and what they may or may not have done.

It is so important during this time to learn how to properly take care of yourself. It is so easy to still be reeling from the abuse that you got in the previous relationship. And instead of taking care of yourself first you become too eager to jump into another relationship and it is often going to be with another narcissist. This is going to start the cycle again.

Of course, there are some targets who are going to take things in a slightly different manner. Instead of being worried about jumping into a new relationship, they are going to spend their time and energy worried that everyone they meet is a narcissist, and that they need to be on constant watch all of the time. this is a hard thing to deal with as well, and it is going to ensure that you will be lonely and isolated from the rest of the group.

Learning who you are as a person, without the narcissist being there, is one of the absolute best things that you are able to do when it comes to getting over the relationship that you had with the narcissist, and when it comes to making sure that you don't just jump right back into another relationship with a new narcissist in the process. Following the tips and suggestions in this chapter are going to help to make this possible.

Chapter 4: How to Pick Out a Good Therapist

As someone who has gone through the abuse that a narcissist can throw out, it is very confusing where to go next. The narcissist probably had a good hold on you for a very long time, and now that you are back out there in the real world, trying to bring yourself out of some of the isolation that you are dealing with, and back into your true self, there are going to be a few road bumps that happen along the way.

Doing it all on your own is going to be almost impossible. It would be nice if you were able to handle the narcissist and all of the physical, mental, and emotional problems that you are going to face now that that relationship is all done.

This is going to be an uphill battle, even if you are able to get some assistance, and figuring out how to deal with all of this is not something that is recommended by most experts for the target.

Whether you are still in the relationship with the narcissist, or you have just gotten out and you are trying to figure out how to lead your life now, you will find that having a good therapist on your side is going to make a huge difference. It can be scary to think about telling a stranger all of the things that went through. You may have already dealt with a lot of people who are mad at you and who don't believe you, and maybe you have been harmed in the past because of asking for help. Since those who are close to you are going to be those who are causing some more of the disbelief and the hurt, so why wouldn't the therapist do the same thing?

The therapist is going to be a specialist that you are able to work with in order to help you to get out of that relationship. It is likely that as a target, you are going to be lost and confused about the whole situation. You are worried about how others perceive them, they feel embarrassed and shame about the situation, and they are still, despite all of this, they are going to still miss the narcissist and wish for the relationship to work again.

When you are looking for a therapist to work with, you first need to make sure that you feel comfortable with them. Therapy is a tough process to go with, and y our therapist is not just there to be your best friend. When you are fantasizing about how great you thought the relationship with the narcissist was, the therapist may have to come in and be a bit harsh to convince you that it wasn't all that great.

With that said, you still need to find someone who respects you and who isn't going to try and take over the conversation, belittle you, or do anything ese that is going to cause you harm along the way. you need to feel that, even if the therapist has to pull you into reality a bit, that they are on your side, that they respect you, and that they are going to be there to actually help you. If they are not able to do that, and you just don't feel comfortable with them, then it is time to find someone else to work with.

If you are working with a therapist and you don't feel like you are getting any relief from those emotional problems in your life, then it is likely that you aren't getting the best treatment that is available. Look for a few warning signs to tell if it is time to get out there and choose a different therapist to work with, such as them not respecting you, then not listening, and more.

The second thing to look for is to find a therapist who has some experience. Dealing with the emotional, mental, and physical signs of something as big as narcissistic abuse is going to be hard, and you want to make sure you go with someone who has the experience to take care of you and actually help you out. For these kinds of cases, it is often best to find someone who has been practicing as a therapist for ten years or more. The longer that a therapist has been practicing in the field, the better the outcome for the client.

This means that if you go with someone who has the right kind of experience behind them, then they are more likely to actually help you. You can seek out someone who has specific experience with the issue, because it can go poorly if you are the first time that the therapist has dealt with that particular issue. But working with someone who knows how to handle your case can make a world of difference.

When you are talking with the therapist, remember that you need to open up, and not be shy. This can be hard after all the issues with the narcissist, but this is the only way that they are going to be able to help you. Remember that you are going to be interviewing your therapist as much as they are interviewing you.

You should ask a lot of questions, especially during the first session with them including

1. How long have you been in practice?
2. have you seen a lot of clients with similar concerns as my own?
3. When was the last time you treated someone with a problem that is similar to mine?

And any other questions that come into your head or you are concerned about should be brought up during this timing as well. You want to make sure that you are picking out the right therapist for your needs, and that they are going to be able to take care of you.

The next thing to consider here is whether you are able to afford a therapist or not. If you are not able to afford a psychologist, which would be the best option to help you get through this kind of situation, then you can work with a social worker.

These individuals may have a bit less training and experience than the other, but after they are in the field for some time, this is going to become less noticeable because they are going to handle a lot of cases. They are becoming more and more prevalent in giving psychotherapy because the field of managed care is growing so much in recent years.

A couple of things you should note here though. It seems like clients are not really seeing much of a difference between the different types of therapists that they use. The results that are coming in are going to be pretty similar. As long as you find someone who has experience in your field, and someone you are comfortable with, you are going to be just fine working with anyone.

So, the next thing to look at is how you are going to choose a therapist to get started with, no matter what their degree is. the answer of this is going to depend many times on the insurance that you have, if you plan to use this there are some insurance companies and HMOs that are going to first need to talk to their GP and then get a referral from that person, before you are able to find any kind of therapist you will need to take a look at the benefits that come with your own insurance in order to figure out how you need to go about this. If you don't go through the process in the proper manner, it means that you will end up with having to pay out of pocket.

From here, the procedure can be hard. And there is not really an easy way for you to choose a professional, no matter what field you are looking at. If you are in a small area, you may be limited in who you can go with because there aren't a lot of options. In bigger areas, there are going to be some referral agencies who can help you out. Doing a search through the yellow pages can be another way that you will be able to find a therapist who will work for you.

You should also be careful about the qualifications that you find in the therapist. You want to make sure that you find a therapist who is registered and licensed in the state or the territory that they practice in. psychologists, for example, are going to have a valid license before they can list themselves under this category. With clinical social workers, they are going to have more of an "L" in front of the degree.

These individuals are not always going to have a license depending on what state they are in, and they are not required to display the licensure in this format.

If you are uncertain about the education and the licensure of the therapist, then go ahead and ask them about it. No legitimate therapist should have a problem with you checking on their educational and professional backgrounds.

If the therapist does have a degree of some sort for the field they are practicing, it is usually going to follow their name in any advertisement that you see, and in some states, this is actually a law that they have to follow. If you are going with a therapist, it is best if you find someone who has a minimum of a Master's degree in their field.

With this one, especially since you are dealing with the trauma of narcissistic abuse, you want to make sure that you avoid just regular counselors, ones who have little to no formal training at all.

And be careful about any titles that they hold that you are not able to recognize at all. For example, in New York, you just need a high school diploma in order to become what is known as a Certified Addictions Counselor. This may sound pretty impressive, but it is very misleading because there is very little training that is needed in order to get this certificate.

Once you have set up an appointment with your therapist, you will need to go to one of the appointments. You are going to do an Intake Evaluation, which is not going to be the same that you do on all of the other appointments along the way. this one is going to be where you explain what brings you to therapy, what symptoms you are experiencing, and some of your general and family history.

This will take a bit of time, and the amount of depth that they go into will depend on the situation and the therapist. There will be a lot of information that the therapist will use to help understand you and your situation a bit more. They may ask you questions about your childhood, education, social relationships and friends, romantic relationships, your current living situation, and your career.

When the therapist is done with this history, they are going to have a much better understanding of who you are and all of the things that are important and will make up your life. They also know what difficulties are there and where they need to go from there. They will then take some time to see if you have any questions. This is a good time for you to see what approach they have, and any other questions that would make you feel more comfortable working with them in the future.

You may be curious as to how long this whole process is going to take. While this sometimes seems like an easy question, it is actually a hard one to go through. This is because each patient is going to vary based on their own backgrounds, how severe the problem is, and a lot of other factors. For mild problems, it is likely that the treatment is not going to be too long, and will just take 12 to 18 sessions.

But if you are dealing with a severe problem, especially if it is long-term or chronic, then it is going to take you a bit longer. Some therapy can last a year or more based on how long it takes to work on the problem. The choice is always yours though. If you start going to the sessions and feel like you have benefited enough after so long, then you can talk to your therapist about ending the sessions.

A good therapist may question this decision a bit to make sure that you are positive, but they will respect your decision, and they are going to try and get the process all done in a session or two to help you wrap all of it up.

However, you know that you are working with an unprofessional, or even an unethical, therapist, if they start to attack your decision and they want to keep you in therapy for an indefinite amount of time. if you are dealing with this kind of person, you need to be firm, and decide to leave whether they want you to or not. It is hopeful that you will get a good therapist who will understand when you are done and will work to help heal you and let you go, but there are some therapists who are not going to act in an appropriate manner all the time.

Therapy is a great option to work with when it comes to your overall mental and emotional help after dealing with a narcissist. It is sometimes hard to let go of the pain and the hurt that they caused you all that time, but with a good therapist, and with focusing on yourself for some time, you will be able to make it all better and will be able to get your old life back, making sure that the narcissist is no longer able to take over your life.

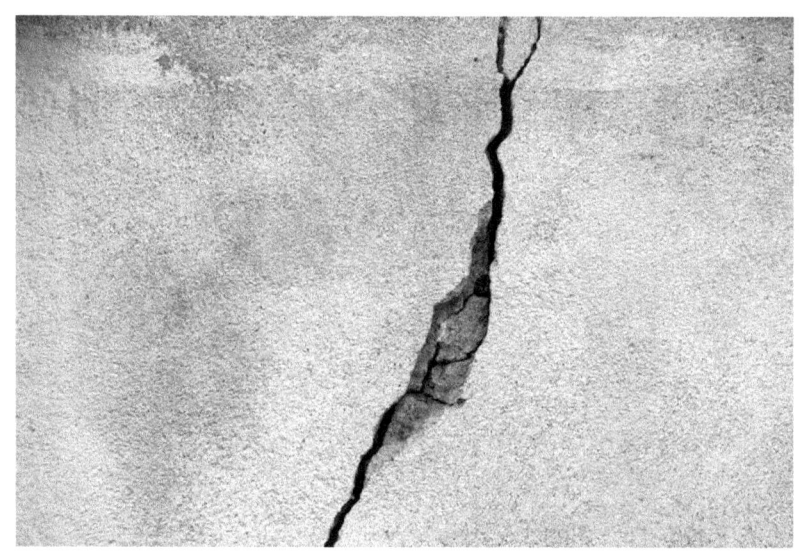

Chapter 5: The Importance of Coming Up with a Good Support Group After Your Narcissistic Relationship

Finding a good support group after you are done with a narcissistic relationship is one of the best things that you can do when it comes to your overall health it will help you to learn how to take care of yourself, and makes it easier to have a social group who is ready and willing to be there to help you through it all.

You may have to spend some time finding this support group, but you will be able to find some people who are willing and able to be that support you need, that shoulder to cry on, and so much more.

The first place you can look to find that support that you need is with your family and friends. You may have to go through and talk about the situation you were in, and how it affected you first. Since you were dealing with a narcissist, and it is likely that you were really isolated for some time, many of those around you are not going to fully know the situation and what was going on with you.

This part can be hard. There are going to be a lot of emotions that come out here, and it is going to start opening you up to the hurt that you were causing to other people along the way. you start to see how isolated you were, how much it hurt other people when you were not responding to them or being mean to them, and so much more.

This is not necessarily a bad thing though. It is good to get things off your chest, and it is good to listen to how others were harmed along the way as well. You may not like it, but this is a great way to help open you up to some of the problems that were going on, and an lead you to the path of healing yourself a bit better.

When you do this, you are going to get some friends and family who understand. They may have seen what was going on and noticed that there was something wrong with your partner from the beginning. Not everyone is going to be fooled by the charisma of a narcissist, and these were probably the people who told you there was something wrong with that person, but you had chosen not to listen. These people are much more likely to come back to you, glad that they get a chance to help and that you are finally free of that toxic relationship.

With that said, you may notice that there are a lot of people who were once in your inner circle, people you were once close to, who are going to run into some troubles with believing you and wanting to have anything to do with you at all. This may sound harsh, and it is going to be hard to deal with. But it is an important thing to keep in mind that it can happen. And you need to allow this to happen. Not everyone is going to understand what you were going through, and some may not even believe you. Right now is about you healing and getting better, and ignoring the others who aren't on your side is best for this time of your life.

There are a number of reasons why people are not going to come back to your side and be your support group. The first of these are the ones who are not going to believe you.

These people have probably met the narcissistic partner at some point and were taken in by their charm as well. They think that you are just trying to mess around or you are just mad that the relationship ended, and you are trying to make the narcissist out to be the bad guy. They are less likely to believe what you are saying, and will decide to side with your ex rather than with you.

And then there are those who are just not able to forgive and forget. They felt that you left them and abandoned them to go chase after some partner, and they were hurt. Maybe you did or said some things, or the narcissist did or said some things, that really hurt them, and they aren't ready to let you back into their life.

Your relationship may have been hard on more than just you. While you do need to take this time to focus on you and getting better so that you can move on in life and get better, you have to realize that others were hurt in the process as well it is perfectly normal for them to not want to do it over again and work with you again.

During this time, even if it does hurt, you need to just let it happen. These people have been hurt as well, and whether or not they believe what you are saying doesn't really matter here. You need to work on yourself as much as possible first. After you have healed from the narcissism and the abuse that you went through, you can go through and try to make up with these relationships if you choose. But in the beginning, you are going to just focus on yourself and the good support group you are able to get in the beginning

Once you have gone through and find the people who are willing to still be on your side, you may find that this only end sup being a few people. That doesn't mean that the cause is a lost one. It just means that you may need to go away from your old inner circle and find some new friends. This is the perfect way to become a bit more social and work hard to get out of the isolation you have been in for some time now due to the narcissist abuser.

For this one, you are going to spend some time going out and doing the things you love. Whether you like to paint, volunteer, write, learn, or do something else, you will be able to find a group of people who want to do it with you as well. Get out into the community and try something new.

You may be surprised at how many people you can meet, and how these can soon become your biggest supporters, and best friends I the process.

There are a lot of support groups out there who will be able to help people with almost any kind of problem they are dealing with, whether it is abuse, cancer, gambling and more. These support groups are defined as being a group of people who have experiences that are similar, and concerns that are similar, and who will get together in order to provide some form of encouragement, advice, and even emotional help. Whether you are going to a formal support group for abuse victims or you are just relying on the friends and family members in your life who have agreed to support you, this is a very good thing.

When you are going through a time that is really emotional, having the support of your peers is going to be super powerful.

This dynamic is going to be even more true when you get out of the abusive relationship. Once you start to realize that you are not the only one going through this situation, it is going to become easier to open up to treatment, to realize how bad things got, and to learn how to let it all go rather than holding on and hoping that things will be better if you go back to that person one more time.

Support groups are not just helpful, they are also going to provide a safe place for us to boune ideas and discuss some of the challenges we face as we try to leave the narcissist and try to start up a new life. Keeping motivated and staying positive is going to be much easier when we are able to turn to others to help us, especially when they have faced, or are facing, the same kinds of challenges as you are.

These support groups can either be nonprofessional or professional. And the treatment that you are given from them can also be informal or formal. In many cases, the support is going to be pretty much essential when it comes to the treatment that you get. But no matter how you do it, it is going to give you the emotional support that you need to ensure you can get through this hard time in your life.

People who are victims of abuse are going to need some help, but so do a lot of the people who are around you.

The impact of that abuse has gone so much further than just you, the one who is dealing with it. There are times with the family and friends are going to feel some anxiety, especially if they were harmed in the relationship at all, or if they knew something was wrong and didn't do anything to stop it or help with it. They may even feel tense when they see that there are signs that you want to go back to the narcissist, or they worry that you are going to get into a relationship with another narcissist at some time.

These are all going to be in conflict with the love and the support that these family members want to give to their loved on. Being able to talk to someone about the problem, either one another or in a support group, can be the best way to solve this problem quickly.

This is a time to open up with others. It is a time to figure out the best way to get to know yourself and understand the situation that was going on around you. Having an actual support group, filled with others who have gone through the abuse as well at some point, is the best option.

These individuals have already gone through the same process that you are now, and so they an talk about what helped them, about their own experience, and so much more. This is going to prove to be invaluable as you try to make it through your own situation.

Take this time to learn as much about the situation and about healing as possible. While this isn't enough to get you out of counseling altogether, and you should still go and talk to a therapist, this can provide you with another level of help as well. The therapist is going to be able to walk you through a lot of the things that you are dealing with emotionally and can give you some tools that will help you to get ahead and see some results quickly.

But it still is not the same thing as talking to others who are in your same situation. The therapist can help quite a bit, but unless they have been through the same kind of abuse as you have, they are not able to fully understand what happened.

Having a good support group, including close friends and family and those who are going through, or who have already gone through, the abuse of narcissists, can be a valuable tool. Make sure that you are an active participant when you go to one of these. Tell your story, ask questions, and learn how you can better cope with the issues that you are dealing with in your life.

Finding a good support group is going to be a great thing to help you get through this abuse. The narcissist did a number on you, trying to ensure that you are not going to run away and try to leave them. It isn't because they actually are about you; it is because it makes their life easier and because they get the attention and more that they want. But when you surround yourself with a lot of support so you can get over the relationship, the power of the narcissist is going to disappear in no time.

Conclusion

Thank for making it through to the end of *Narcissistic Recovery*, let's hope it was informative and able to provide you with all of the tools you need to achieve your goals whatever they may be.

The next step is to get started with the help of narcissistic recovery, so that you are able to leave the narcissist behind, and ensure that you are going to see the best results possible. There are a lot of people who find that they end up in one of these relationships, but they don't know how to escape it at all. The narcissist is often going to do a great job making sure that they won't lose their hold on the target, that it may seem impossible to even try.

This guidebook is going to take some time to look at the different things that you are able to do in order to finally get the recovery that you need. The target is often going to fall in a hard place. They know that the relationship is not a good one for them, but they are going to struggle because they still remember the good times, they still remember they loved the narcissist, and they still don't want to give it up, feeling like they have to rely on the narcissist to help them to do well in life.

The narcissist did a great job making sure that they were able to get into the heads of their victims this way as good as possible. They have no interest in letting that target go, unless they absolutely have to. This makes it even harder for the target to get away because the narcissist is so powerful, and it seems like they are surrounded.

This guidebook took some time to look at the different stages of narcissistic abuse, the stages that the target is able to go through in order to finally end that relationship and get their life back on track, and all of the other things that the target needs to know in order to do well with this whole issue.

Getting away from the narcissist after a bad breakup, and making sure that you are able to protect yourself and get the best results when it comes to healing, can be tough. If you want to help yourself recover from the work that the narcissist did to you, make sure to check out this guidebook to help you to get started.

CPSIA information can be obtained
at www.ICGtesting.com
Printed in the USA
BVHW042340260621
610451BV00004B/895